Martin Luther King Jr.

by Lucia Raatma

Compass Point Early Biographies

Content Adviser: Professor Sherry L. Field,
Department of Social Science Education, College of Education,
The University of Georgia

Reading Adviser: Dr. Linda D. Labbo,
Department of Reading Education, College of Education,
The University of Georgia

✦ **COMPASS POINT BOOKS**
Minneapolis, Minnesota

Compass Point Books
3722 West 50th Street, #115
Minneapolis, MN 55410

Visit Compass Point Books on the Internet at *www.compasspointbooks.com* or e-mail your
request to *custserv@compasspointbooks.com*

Photographs ©: HultonGetty/Archive Photos, cover, cover (background), 5, 7, 9, 11, 15, 16, 21, 22,
23, 24, 25, 26; Wide World/FPG International, 4; Library of Congress, 6, 8, 12, 13, 14, 17; AP/Wide
World Photos, 18; Jeff Mitchell/HultonGetty/Archive Photos, 27.

Editors: E. Russell Primm, Emily J. Dolbear, and Laura Driscoll
Photo Researcher: Svetlana Zhurkina
Photo Selector: Linda S. Koutris
Designer: Bradfordesign, Inc.

Library of Congress Cataloging-in-Publication Data

Raatma, Lucia.
    Martin Luther King Jr. / by Lucia Raatma.
        p. cm. — (Compass Point early biographies)
    Includes bibliographical references and index.
        ISBN 0-7565-0114-8 (hardcover, library binding)
        1. King, Martin Luther Jr., 1929–1968—Juvenile literature. 2. African-Americans—
Biography—Juvenile literature. 3. Civil rights workers—United States—Biography—Juvenile litera-
ture. 4. Baptists—United States—Clergy—Biography—Juvenile literature. 5. African-Americans—
Civil rights—History—20th century—Juvenile literature. [1. King, Martin Luther, Jr., 1929_1968. 2.
Civil rights workers. 3. Clergy. 4. Civil rights movements—History. 5. African-Americans—
Biography.] I. Title. II. Series.
    E185.97.K5 R27 2002
    323'.092—dc21
2001001578

Table of Contents

A Worker for Change

Martin Luther King Jr. was a great speaker and leader. He lived at an important time in the United States.

Many laws were unfair to African-Americans then. Martin Luther King Jr. worked hard to change these laws.

Martin Luther King Jr. was a great speaker.

 Martin Luther King Jr.

Growing Up in the South

Martin Luther King Jr. was born on January 15, 1929. He was born in Atlanta, Georgia. His father was a **minister** at a church.

Life was different for blacks then. In southern

The city of Atlanta around the time that Martin Luther King Jr. was born

states, laws kept whites and blacks apart. These laws were called **segregation** laws. Segregation means "keep separate."

These laws meant that blacks and whites could not go to the same schools. They could not sit in the same parts of cafés. Some beaches, parks, and hotels were

Unfair laws kept blacks out of many places.

for "whites only." African-Americans could not enter them.

Many people thought these laws were unfair. Martin's father was one of these people. Martin heard him talk about it often. Maybe this is why young Martin hated these laws too.

School and College

Martin was a very good student. He skipped two grades in school! He went to **college**

Martin Luther King Jr. speaking in church

when he was only fifteen years old.

After college, Martin went to another school to learn about religion. He became a minister just like his father.

In school, Martin Luther King Jr. learned about a man named Mahatma Gandhi. Gandhi was a leader in India. He believed in trying to

change things
that were wrong.
He always spoke
out in peaceful
ways. He did
not believe in
fighting.

Martin Luther
King Jr. liked
Gandhi's ideas.
He thought black
people could use
them to change
the laws in the
South.

Mahatma Gandhi

Starting a Family

When Martin Luther King Jr. was twenty-four years old, he married Coretta Scott. She was from Alabama.

Martin and Coretta lived in Montgomery, Alabama. Over the years, they had four children.

Martin Luther King Jr. became the minister of a church in Montgomery. In church, he talked to the people about God. He also talked about working to get equal rights for black people.

Meanwhile, Martin Luther King Jr. was

Martin Luther King Jr. with his wife, Coretta, and one of their children

studying even more. He earned a special degree called a **doctorate**. From then on, he was known as Dr. King. It did not mean that he was a medical doctor. It meant that he was a very educated man.

The Battle over Buses

December 1, 1955, was a big day in Montgomery. A black woman named Rosa Parks was riding on a bus.

At that time, blacks had to sit in the back of the buses. Only whites could sit up front. When the back seats were full, blacks had to stand.

The bus driver told Rosa Parks to stand. She said no. So the police took her to jail.

This made many people angry. The black people of Montgomery wanted to do something about it.

Rosa Parks was fingerprinted in jail.

They came up with a plan. They would not ride the buses until the bus company changed its rules.

The people formed a group. They chose Dr. King as their leader. They knew he could help them stand up for what was right.

Not everyone in Montgomery agreed with Dr. King, however. Some whites did not want blacks to have equal rights. They tried to scare Dr. King.

One night, his home was bombed. Luckily, no one was hurt.

Finally, in December 1956, the Supreme Court of the United

Dr. King was a popular leader in Montgomery.

13

States gave an order. The Court said that the Montgomery bus system had to treat all its riders the same way. It was a big win for Dr. King and his friends.

Dr. King was put in jail for his work against the Montgomery bus company.

Leading Others

When Dr. King was thirty years old, he and his family left Montgomery. They moved to Atlanta, Georgia. Dr. King worked with his father at his church.

Dr. King was becoming well known. Many white people also agreed with his ideas.

In the next few years, Dr. King gave many

Blacks and whites marched with Dr. King.

speeches. He told black people to fight for change. He told them to fight with words, not with their fists.

Dr. King led marches through towns. The marches showed that many people wanted things to change.

Black students and white students began to hold **sit-ins**. In cafés, they sat down in the "white only" areas. They would not move to the "black" areas.

◄ At a sit-in in Maryland

Dr. King was put into jail after the march in Birmingham, Alabama.

Sometimes Dr. King joined in the sit-ins. Many of the students and Dr. King were taken to jail. But they were ready for that. They felt they were doing what was right. Over the years, Dr. King was put in jail about thirty times.

During one march in Birmingham, Alabama, the police got very rough. They wanted to stop

the march. They used dogs to control the marchers. They used huge water hoses.

Reporters took pictures. The pictures showed African-Americans being attacked by dogs and sprayed by water. The pictures were on the news. They were printed in newspapers.

More and more people—both black and white—got angry. They agreed that blacks should have equal rights.

Police dogs attacking marchers

Talking to the Nation

John F. Kennedy, the president, also started listening to Dr. King. President Kennedy tried to help Dr. King in his work.

The president wanted to pass a new law. It would protect the rights of all people.

In 1963, black leaders planned a march in Washington, D.C., the nation's capital. It is the place where laws are made. At the march, they would demand equal rights and better jobs for blacks.

More than 250,000 Americans joined in the march. Many more watched on television. There were marchers of all colors and all

Giving the "I Have a Dream" speech

ages. They marched from one part of
Washington to another. Then they listened to
many speeches.

Martin Luther King gave a famous speech
that day. It was called the "I Have a Dream"
speech. He talked about his hopes for America.

21

Dr. King watches President Johnson sign the Civil Rights Act of 1964.

He wanted blacks and whites to be equal. He wanted them to be at peace.

The speech was so moving that many people cried. They knew it was a great moment in history.

The next year, Congress passed a law. It was called the Civil Rights Act of 1964. It said that no one could be kept out of any public place because of his or her race.

Marching On

A year later, Martin Luther King took part in another march. He wanted to speak out about voting rights. At the

In 1964, Dr. King received a great award, the Nobel Peace Prize, for his work.

time, black people had the right to vote. But unfair rules sometimes kept them from voting.

The march began in a town called Selma, Alabama. It would end in Montgomery, the state capital.

At first, police stopped the march. They used clubs and other weapons. More than seventy marchers were hurt.

Marching from Selma to Montgomery for voting rights

Two weeks later, a court said that the march could go on. A group of 3,000 marchers made the trip. It took five days. At the end, thousands of people were waiting to hear Martin Luther King speak.

Soon Congress passed another law. It made it easier for blacks to vote in the South. The new law was another big win.

A Better Life

Martin Luther King Jr. continued to fight for equal rights. Some people thought the battle was won. But Dr. King knew there was still **racism** against black people. The new laws gave blacks more rights. But many blacks were still poor.

Dr. King fought for better jobs, better schools, and better homes. He wanted all Americans to have a chance at a better life.

Dr. King gave many speeches during his life.

A Man of Peace

In 1968, Dr. King visited Memphis, Tennessee. He was there to talk to a group of black workers. On April 4, he was standing outside his motel room. Gunfire rang out and Dr. King was shot. Less than an hour later, he died in a hospital.

James Earl Ray

Police caught a man named James Earl Ray. Some say that Ray did not kill Dr. King on his own. They say others worked with him. No one knows for sure.

The death of Martin Luther King Jr. was a great loss. He lived his life to serve others.

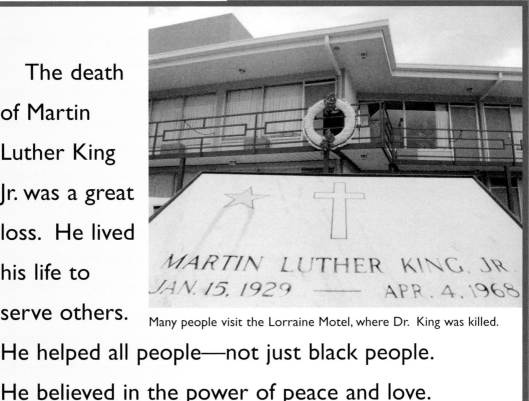

Many people visit the Lorraine Motel, where Dr. King was killed.

He helped all people—not just black people. He believed in the power of peace and love. He gave hope to the poor and powerless everywhere.

In the United States today, Martin Luther King Jr. is a national hero. He is honored each year on the third Monday in January. That day is known as Martin Luther King Jr. Day.

Important Dates in Martin Luther King Jr.'s Life

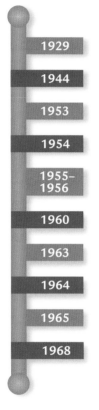

1929	Born on January 15 in Atlanta, Georgia
1944	Enters college at age fifteen
1953	Marries Coretta Scott
1954	Becomes a minister in Montgomery, Alabama
1955–1956	Leads the fight against the Montgomery bus system
1960	Gets support from President John F. Kennedy
1963	Gives his "I Have a Dream" speech in Washington, D.C.
1964	Wins the Nobel Peace Prize
1965	Marches from Selma to Montgomery, Alabama, to speak out about voting rights for blacks
1968	Shot and killed on April 4 in Memphis, Tennessee

Glossary

college—a place to continue learning after high school

doctorate—the highest degree given by a college or university

minister—the leader of a church

racism—the belief that one race is better than others

segregation—keeping races of people apart from one another

sit-ins—peaceful protests in which people sit in one place and refuse to leave

Did You Know?

- Martin Luther King's family called him "M.L."

- The motel in Memphis where Martin Luther King was killed is now home to the National Civil Rights Museum.

- Martin Luther King Jr. Day was first celebrated in 1986.

Want to Know More?

At the Library

Bull, Angela. *Free at Last! The Story of Martin Luther King Jr.* New York: DK Publishing, 2000.

Friskey, Margaret. *What Is Martin Luther King Jr. Day?* Chicago: Children's Press, 1990.

Marzollo, Jean. *Happy Birthday, Martin Luther King.* New York: Scholastic Trade, 1993.

Schaefer, Lola M. *Martin Luther King Jr.* Mankato, Minn.: Pebble Books, 1999.

On the Web

Archer Audio Archives—Dr. Martin Luther King Jr.
http://www.archervalerie.com/mlk.html
For audio files of some of Dr. King's speeches

Martin Luther King Jr.: A Life Tribute
http://www.lifemag.com/Life/mlk/mlk.html
For photos of Dr. King that appeared in *Life* magazine

Through the Mail

The Martin Luther King Jr.'s Center for Nonviolent Social Change
449 Auburn Avenue, N.E.
Atlanta, GA 30312
To get more information about how Dr. King worked to change the
world in a peaceful way

On the Road

The National Civil Rights Museum
450 Mulberry Street (in the Lorraine Motel)
Memphis, TN 38103-4214
901/521-9699
To learn more about the civil rights movement and to visit the place
where Dr. King was killed

Index

About the Author

Lucia Raatma received her bachelor's degree in English literature from the University of South Carolina and her master's degree in cinema studies from New York University. She has written a wide range of books for young people. When she is not researching or writing, she enjoys going to movies, playing tennis, and spending time with her husband, daughter, and golden retriever. She lives in New York.